PAUL S

ALIEN
Bek

Illustrated by
Anthony Lewis

OXFORD
UNIVERSITY PRESS

OXFORD
UNIVERSITY PRESS

Great Clarendon Street, Oxford OX2 6DP

Oxford University Press is a department of the University of Oxford.
It furthers the University's objective of excellence in research, scholarship,
and education by publishing worldwide in

Oxford New York

Athens Auckland Bangkok Bogotá Buenos Aires Calcutta
Cape Town Chennai Dar es Salaam Delhi Florence Hong Kong Istanbul
Karachi Kuala Lumpur Madrid Melbourne Mexico City Mumbai
Nairobi Paris São Paulo Shanghai Singapore Taipei Tokyo Toronto Warsaw

and associated companies in Berlin Ibadan

Oxford is a trade mark of Oxford University Press
in the UK and in certain other countries

British Library Cataloguing in Publication Data
Data available

ISBN 0 19 915951 3

Printed in Hong Kong

Available in packs

Year 4 / Primary 5 Pack of Six (one of each book)   ISBN 0 19 915955 6
Year 4 / Primary 5 Class Pack (six of each book)   ISBN 0 19 915956 4

for Anna

Contents

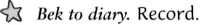 *Bek to diary.* Record.
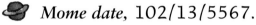 *Mome date,* 102/13/5567.
Earth date, 28 August; a.m.

Well, I'm here! After all the preparations and delays, I have finally made it to Planet Earth.

I can't wait to meet my first humans. After all, they are the life-forms I have been sent to study. My year-long mission on Earth is to find out about what Earth people call "feelings" - and, if possible, to experience them.

I told Dibs to drop me off somewhere with lights. But would

she listen? Would she stardust!

☆ "Bright lights mean danger," she said.

☆ So here I am, in the middle of nowhere, in full human disguise. There are meant to be more than six billion humans on the planet. You'd think I could find just one!

☆ I've been walking since dawn. Yellow stalks with seedstuff are swaying high above my head all round me. I knew that Earth is a fertile planet, but...

☆ *Beep-beep-beep-beep-beep!*

☆ Uh-oh! My alarm is signalling danger. I am under attack from a huge creature. It's loud. It's heavy. And it's heading this way...

Diary, close.

1

Greetings!

Olly stood on the fence at the back of his house, watching Farmer Butterworth driving round and round his wheat field.

"Harvest time, already," Olly thought. "School again next week."

Not that Olly minded. Living out in the country meant that he hardly ever got to see his friends in the holidays.

He was looking forward to the new term.

When only a small circle of wheat remained in the centre of the field, Farmer Butterworth switched off the

engine of the combine harvester and beeped his horn. Dozens of small animals – mice, rats and rabbits, snakes and toads – scurried across the field to the safety of the woods beyond.

Suddenly, the combine harvester glowed a dazzling blue. Farmer Butterworth screamed.

Without a second thought, Olly jumped over the fence and raced towards it. "Farmer Butterworth," he shouted. "Are you all right?"

From behind him came a voice. "You know this curious creature?" it said.

Olly spun round. His jaw dropped. Before him stood a small man wearing a silver spacesuit and pink tutu, and carrying a zap gun. His hair was dark, his skin pale.

"Greetings!" he said, lifting his visor. "My name's Bek."

Too surprised to be frightened, Olly stared at the doll-sized man in dumb amazement.

"Greetings!" the man repeated. "My..."

"You killed Farmer Butterworth," said Olly.

Bek frowned. "The creature has a name?" he said.

"The creature?" said Olly.

Bek peered inside the combine harvester and saw a bearded human slumped against the steering wheel. "Oh," he said. "I thought..." He shrugged. "Still, no harm done. He'll come round in ten Earth minutes and he won't remember a thing."

Olly stared in confusion. "Who are you?" he said.

"I told you, my name's Bek…"

"But…" Olly began.

Bek sighed. "They've got the size wrong, haven't they?" he said. "Tell me I'm too small."

"You are rather on the short side," Olly agreed.

"I knew it!" said Bek. "Those black-holes-for-brains back on Mome must have put the decimal point in the wrong place! What am I expected to do now?" He paused. "I don't suppose you could give me a hand, could you?"

☆ *Bek to diary.* Record.

🪐 *Mome date,* 102/13/5569.

🌑 *Earth date,* 28 August; p.m.

☆ *Vocabulary update:* Wheat.
   Combine harvester. Farmer.
   Spaghetti bolognaise.

☆ Given the fact that I'm about a
tenth of the size I should be, things
are going well. I have met my first
human. He is called Oliver Ross -
but he says I can call him Olly. He is
asleep now. I am lying at the
bottom of his bed.

☆   I've told him everything. Since it
is impossible for me to blend in

with the crowd, I had to enlist the help of someone I can trust. Oliver - Olly - seems a good choice.

 He tells me that, because I am the size of a doll, I must act as one. Whenever his birth-mother or other human being appears I must lie still.

So far, I have observed three important human emotions. *Concern* - when Olly saw Farmer Butterworth sitting so still. *Relief* - when I told him he would be all right. And *delight* - when he found he had spaghetti bolognaise for tea.

Interesting!
Diary, close.

2

Into Town

Olly woke up at six on the dot, as he had every day of the summer holiday. He stared up at the ceiling.

"What a weird dream," he said.

"Dream?" came a voice. "Please, explain."

Olly sat bolt upright. "Bek?" he said.

"Olly?" said Bek.

Olly shook his head. It hadn't been a dream after all. "A real alien," he said.

"I just can't believe this is happening."

Bek stared at his tiny body. "Me neither," he said. He looked up. "You haven't forgotten your promise, have you?"

"No," said Olly. "I'll look after you – and I'll try to help you as much as I can. We'll take the bus into town. You can start your observations there."

"Thank you, Olly," said Bek seriously.

Olly wrote a note for his mum, telling her he'd popped into Ashley. Then, after a hurried breakfast of tea and strawberry jam on toast, he put Bek inside his backpack and the pair of them set off for the bus stop.

"Get down," Olly whispered to Bek as the bus appeared. "And don't make a sound."

Olly climbed on. He placed the bag on the seat so that Bek could peek all round.

It took ages to get to town.

"Flipping traffic jam," the old woman in front muttered.

"It gets worse and worse," an old man agreed.

By the time Olly got off outside the town hall, Bek was bursting with questions. "What...? Who...? How...?" he demanded.

"Shhh!" Olly hissed. "Someone'll hear you."

He went across the road and into Ashley Park. Apart from a woman with a small girl feeding the ducks, the park was deserted. Olly sat down on a bench. Bek climbed out of the backpack.

"Those people on the bus," he said. "Their skin was crinkled. Their hair was white – those who *had* hair."

"They were just old," said Olly.

"Old," said Bek thoughtfully. He paused. "And another thing," he added. "We had strawberry jam for breakfast. But what was that traffic jam everyone was talking about?"

Olly laughed. "It's…"

There was a sound of loud jeering. Olly looked up.

"Oh, no," he moaned. It was Vince Burgess and his two horrible mates, Des and Del.

"Oy, Yokel!" Vince yelled.

"Yokel?" said Bek.

"Ssh!" Olly whispered. "And get inside the backpack before they…"

"If you're trying to hide your dolly, you're too late," said Vince, striding towards him.

"Sissy," said Des.

"Woosy," said Del.

"It… it's an Action Man," said Olly.

"Yeah, yeah," sneered Vince. "With that hair and those clothes! More like Barbie's disco boyfriend." He seized the backpack and dashed off with it.

Olly gave chase. "Give it back!" he yelled.

Vince chucked the bag to Des, who lobbed it to Del, who tossed it back to Vince. Olly's heart thumped. He'd promised to look after Bek!

"Give it back!"

Vince stopped and turned on him.

"Make me," he snarled, and shoved Olly backwards so hard he fell to the ground. Des and Del sniggered unpleasantly. Olly watched as Vince opened the top of the backpack.

"I wouldn't do that," he said.

"Why not?" said Vince. "Dangerous dolly, is it?" he said.

"Yes," said Olly, simply.

For a moment, Vince paused. Then, with a sneer on his lips, he thrust his hand inside.

"Aaaaaarrgh!" he screamed.

A blue light lit up his body. The next instant, he fell to the ground. Des and Del turned on their heels and dashed off.

Bek's head popped up from the top of the bag.

"Are you all right?" said Olly.

"Fine," said Bek. "Though that boy's going to wake up with a headache."

Olly smiled. It was the first time he'd ever got the better of Vince. "He was right about one thing, though," he said. "You do need new clothes!"

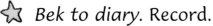 *Bek to diary.* Record.
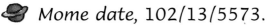 *Mome date,* 102/13/5573.
Earth date, 29 August; p.m.

Vocabulary update: dream,
strawberry jam (edible), traffic
jam (inedible), doll, yokel, army
uniform.

It's been an interesting day. Unlike
Mome, where we are constantly
rejuvenated, Earth people grow old -
their hair loses its colour, their
bones break and their wobbly bits
inside turn to jelly.

    This morning, Olly was attacked

by three boys who were bigger and stronger than him. I taught them a lesson.

 Olly has dressed me up like a soldier. He says that it is just about all right for an eight-year old male child to go round with a doll - so long as it is dressed in army uniform.

This is indeed a strange planet.

I observed more human emotions in Olly. *Fear* - when Vince first appeared. *Anger* - when Vince stole his backpack. And something called *embarrassment*. It made Olly's ears turn red!

Very curious!

Diary, close.

3
Off to School

"You don't seem your normal self," said Bek.

Olly groaned. "I've got a test at school," he said. "And I haven't done any work for it."

"Hmm," said Bek. "This is my fault. You've been helping me so much that you've neglected your own studies."

It was true. Every spare moment had been spent taking Bek to different

places. The market. The zoo. The
museum. The cinema. There was
certainly no time for homework. Olly
had only been back at school four
weeks and already his marks were
down.

"I'll be all right," he said, as he
made for the door. "I'll see you later."

"Yes," said Bek
thoughtfully. "Yes,
you will."

An hour later Olly was at his table,
staring at the test paper in front of
him. They were called lightning tests;
twenty questions from the topics the
class had covered over the previous
month. Mrs Brody believed they kept
her pupils on their toes.

1   *What is the capital of Australia?*
2   *What is 16,445 divided by 23?*
3   *Draw an annotated sketch of an ant...*

And so it went on. Question after unanswerable question.

"What *is* the capital of Australia," Olly muttered. "Sydney? Melbourne?"

He had decided to go for Sydney, when he heard a familiar voice. "Canberra," it said.

"Bek?" Olly gasped. He looked in his backpack.

"I wanted to help you with your test," Bek explained softly.

"Oliver Ross," snapped Mrs Brody. "Close your bag at once. This is a test. No books and no calculators..."

"I... I was just looking for my ruler," Olly stammered.

"Humph!" said Mrs Brody. She

stormed over to his table and opened his bag.

Olly gasped. If she found Bek... He looked down.

There was the usual mess of books, and on top of it all, his ruler.

The rest of the class giggled.

"Get on with your work, all of you," said Mrs Brody. She turned to Olly. "I'll be watching you, Oliver Ross," she said.

Olly stared back at the test paper, and sighed. The only way to get Mrs Brody off his back was to do well in the test. He lay his head down on the crook of his arm, with his ear almost touching the table.

"Bek," he whispered. "How's your long division?"

☆ ☆ ☆

When the bell went for dinner time, everyone handed in their papers as they left the class. No one was allowed to take their bags – so there was no way for Olly to move Bek to somewhere safer.

"Just stay where you are," he

whispered, as he left his seat.

"Mmmff," came the muffled reply.

Olly could only hope that the "mmmff" meant *yes*. School was far too dangerous for a pint-sized alien – zap gun or no zap gun!

Olly was first back in the class after the break. He ran to his bag, tore it open and...

"Bek!" he cried, and rummaged through the books.

But Bek was not there. The "mmmff" had meant *no*, after all.

It was science that afternoon.

Normally, it was Olly's favourite subject, but today all he could think about was the missing alien. What if he'd been chucked into the incinerator or got washed down the drains? What if Sabre, the school cat, had got him? Where was he?

At last, the bell rang for the end of school. Olly stayed behind when everyone else had gone. He searched all round. But Bek was not there.

Olly made his way to the cloakroom. He felt terrible. He'd let the little alien down.

"I'm sorry, Bek," he muttered.

"What for?" came a voice from the coat on his peg.

"Bek?" said Olly.

The alien's head poked up out of the pocket. Olly frowned.

"Bek!" he said crossly. "Why didn't you stay in the bag?"

"I wanted to look round," said Bek. He paused. "I've observed a great deal – and, after all, that's why I'm here."

☆ *Bek to diary.* Record.
🪐 *Mome date,* 103/12/5725.
🌑 *Earth date,* 11 October; p.m.

☆ If all days were like today, I would
be able to return to Mome in time
for Mome New Year. I went to Olly's
school (Ashley Juniors) and observed
so many examples of strange human
behaviour that I hardly know where
to begin.

☆   Two boys hit another boy and
stole his chocolate bar. This is
called *bullying.* Three girls were
mimicking another girl's lisp. This

is called *teasing*. Twelve children played a game where they gradually formed a long chain and chased round the playground. This is called *chain-it*.

☆ In the dining hall, Vince Burgess flicked a spoonful of syrup pudding (very nice with custard) at Olly. This is called *bad manners*.

☆ Olly had something called a lightning test. I gave him all the answers. And this, he told me, is called *cheating*.

☆ Strange. On Mome, we are taught to share information.

Diary, close. ⚡

4

Firework Night

The weeks passed, half-term came and went. Olly could hardly remember what life was like before the miniature alien appeared.

He and Bek went everywhere together – to the swimming baths, the ice rink, the skateboard park. Often, Olly brought home library books, CD-ROMs and videos for Bek to study while he was at school. And at night, Olly tuned the radio in to foreign stations so that the alien could learn about life on other parts of Earth.

One Saturday morning he woke to hear the radio making a curious *doodly-blip* noise. Bek was sitting beside it. He looked tired and pale.

"What's the matter?" said Olly.

Bek looked up. "I re-jigged the radio," he said. "This is a broadcast from Mome. Of course," he added, "it's several thousand years old, but..." He sighed. "I feel so *strange*," he said. "My stomach, my head, my heart...!"

"Oh, no!" said Olly. "I hope you're not getting flu."

"Flu?" said Bek. "*Wuuurgh*," he groaned and lay back on the bed. "Let's stay at home today."

Olly covered him with a blanket.

"On Mome, I'd be put in a healthy-box," said Bek. "We never get ill."

"Hmph," said Olly. "Well, since we won't be going out anywhere today, you can watch me make my guy."

Olly sat up. "Guy?" he said.

"For Firework Night," said Olly. "It's tomorrow. I told you all about it."

"Ah, yes," said Bek. "Guy Fawkes and the Gunpowder Plot to blow up the Houses of Parliament in Earth year 1605."

"Exactly," said Olly. "Mum said I can have a firework party. Here. She's arranging for a coach to bring my whole class over. I need to make a guy for the top of the bonfire." He grinned. "I can't wait. I love fireworks – especially the rockets."

"Rockets?" said Bek quietly. He was beginning to feel better already.

Olly and Bek spent all morning making the guy. It was a beauty! And when it was finished they went out to get everything else ready.

They filled flowerpots with sand for the silver rain and Roman candles, and sank lengths of drainpipe into the

ground for the rockets. They dragged a
heavy metal box for the fireworks
from the shed. Last but not least, they
built the bonfire.

Olly had already been collecting logs
and branches for some while. Piece by
piece, the pair of them built the bonfire
in Farmer Butterworth's top field.

"It looks like a wigwam," said Olly.

"Shouldn't that be a twigwam?"
said Bek.

Olly laughed as he secured the guy
into place. It was good to have Bek
back to his normal self.

Finally, the big day arrived. The fifth of
November. Olly and his mum had just
finished wrapping the scrubbed
potatoes in foil when the coach pulled
up in front of the house. Thirty-three
excited boys and girls jumped out.

Olly slipped on his backpack with
Bek already safely inside, and went out

to join them. Everyone was there – even Des, Del and Vince Burgess. Since the incident in the park they'd stopped calling him Yokel.

With Olly's mum leading the way, they set off for Farmer Butterworth's top field – where Olly had first found Bek all those weeks ago. He smiled, "It seems such a long time."

"I know," Bek sighed.

Dan Butterworth was standing next to the unlit bonfire, a burning torch in his hand. "There you are," he said. "And what a wonderful night for a firework party!"

Olly looked up. The stars were brighter than he'd ever seen them. Even Mome – that distant twinkle that Bek had so often pointed out – looked nearer this evening. "Are you okay back there?" he whispered.

"Yes," Bek whispered back.

"Come on, Olly," said Farmer Butterworth. "You can light the bonfire."

Olly stepped forwards. He took the blazing torch and tossed it on to the tall stack of wood. With a loud *woof*! the whole lot exploded into flames. A cheer went up.

"Let the fireworks begin," Farmer Butterworth announced.

Within seconds the night sky was full of flashes of colour, whines, whizzes and bangs. Everyone ooohed and aaahed. "What do you think?" Olly whispered over his shoulder.

There was no answer.

"Bek, there's no need to be frightened," he said.

But still Bek did not reply.

Suddenly Olly was struck by an awful thought. He tore off the backpack. It was empty.

"Bek," he gasped.

He ran this way and that, looking for the tiny alien. But Bek was nowhere to be found.

"And now," Farmer Butterworth shouted above the noise of the spinning Catherine wheels. "For the finale, the biggest rocket I could find. I give you, Star Seeker."

A hush fell. The rocket was a monster! The children watched open-mouthed as Farmer Butterworth lit the blue touch-paper.

Olly looked around. At the bonfire. On the ground. Where was Bek?

The Star Seeker hissed.

Olly spun round and...

WHOOSH!
The rocket soared
up into the sky.
"YEAH!" screamed
thirty-three children.
"No," Olly gasped,
as the tiny alien he'd seen
strapped to the stick of the
rocket abruptly disappeared.
"Bek!" he cried.
Higher and higher the
rocket went, before exploding
with a bang and a shower of
golden sparks – then red,
then green, then blue and
silver.
It crackled and whined.
It glittered and flashed.
Suddenly, a deafening

BOOM! echoed
round the starlit sky.

The firework display
was over. And so, Olly
knew, was Bek.

Unless…

It was a long shot, but
Bek had been dressed in his
spaceman gear. If it was
fireproof…

Olly scanned the sky for
any trace of the little alien. He
noticed something far away
to his left. Something falling.
Something white. Without a
second thought, Olly took
to his heels.

He raced across the
field, leapt a ditch,
jumped a stile and

continued through a meadow full of cows. The white thing was still ahead of him. It was coming down far too slowly to be a bit of the rocket.

Suddenly, it was directly over his head. Olly reached out and caught the falling object in his hands.

It was Bek.

His parachute had stopped him from plummeting to earth – but it had opened too late for the little alien.

"Oh, Bek," Olly sobbed as he hugged the lifeless little alien to his chest. "Why?" he howled. *"Why?"*

"Because," came a tiny voice.

Olly held the doll-sized figure out in front of him. Bek's hand moved shakily to his helmet, and lifted the visor.

"I've been stupid, haven't I?" he said.

☆ *Bek to diary*. Record.
🪐 *Mome date*, 104/05/5825.
🌑 *Earth date*, 5 November; p.m.

☆ *Vocabulary Update:*
　　Guy Fawkes Night,
　　rocket (meaning 2: a firework),
　　bonfire, jacket potatoes (nothing
　　to do with clothes!)

☆ What can I say? I have acted in a
way I have never acted before. I
cannot explain my behaviour.

☆ 　At 20:33 Earth time I attempted
to return to Mome. Even though I

knew the rocket was far too primitive to complete the journey, something told me I had to try.

What on earth is happening to me?

I have observed and identified more human emotions. *Excitement* - when Olly was talking about the fireworks. *Pride* - when he lit the bonfire. *Grief* - when he thought I was dead. (His eyes leaked water.) I...

Oh, but what's the point?

Diary, close.

5

Mome Sweet Mome

"What were you doing?" said Olly.

"I… errm…" said Bek. He looked up. "What did you hear?"

"Everything," said Olly.

Bek nodded. "Then you know my real reason for being here," he said. "It's not just to explore Earth, but to study human emotions. There are no such things on Mome, you see. The problem is, although I can now identify them in others – fear, anger, pride, excitement – I cannot experience them myself. I have failed in my mission!"

Olly smiled. "But you *have* felt a human emotion," he said. "I'm sure of it."

"I have?" said Bek.

"When you were listening to the radio broadcast from Mome," he said, "you felt an empty, knotted feeling in your stomach, didn't you?"

"Yes," said Bek.

"Your head thumped. Your heart ached…"

"Yes, yes," said Bek.

"You weren't ill at all," said Olly.

"I wasn't?"

"No," said Olly. "You felt homesick!"

"Felt… homesick," said Bek, slowly.

"And that made me act so stupidly."
His face broke into a smile.
"Momesick, more like!" he said.

"Mome is where the heart is!" said
Olly. They were both laughing now.
"Mome, Sweet Mome!"

Bek looked up. "Olly," he said.
"How does it feel inside when you like
someone?"

"Sort of warm and light and
comfortable," said Olly.

Bek nodded. "Then I must say
something I have never once said to
anyone on Mome, Olly. I like you a
lot."

"And I like you, too," said Olly.

"My second human emotion!" said
Bek. "Perhaps my teacher won't fail
me, after all."

Olly smiled. It was odd to imagine
an alien version of Mrs Brody on the

faraway planet. "And you've still got nearly three hundred more Earth days before you must return," said Olly. "Loads of time to experience all kinds of other emotions."

Bek nodded – happily. "I'm glad," he said.

"So am I, Bek," said Olly. "Night night."

"Good night, Olly," said Bek. "My friend."

About the author

I've had lots of jobs. I've worked in a bank, a record shop and several language schools, from Germany to Sri Lanka.

Now I live in Brighton with my wife and two children. I spend the days doing what I always wanted to do most – writing books.

I've written more than forty so far, from picture books and football stories, to fantasy and horror novels.

Alien Bek started out as a dream. I think I must have eaten too much cheese before going to bed that night!